DATE DUE

GAYLORD			PRINTED IN U.S.A.

OCT   2003

FROM SEA TO SHINING SEA

OKLAHOMA

LINDA SAYLOR-MARCHANT

Consultants

MELISSA N. MATUSEVICH, PH.D.

Curriculum and Instruction Specialist
Blacksburg, Virginia

BETTIE ESTES-RICKNER

Director, Information Technology Services
Putnam City Schools
Oklahoma City, Oklahoma

JENNY FOSTER STENIS

Children's Services Manager
Moore Public Library
Pioneer Library System

CHILDREN'S PRESS®

A DIVISION OF SCHOLASTIC INC.

New York • Toronto • London • Auckland • Sydney • Mexico City
New Delhi • Hong Kong • Danbury, Connecticut

Oklahoma is located in the interior plains of the United States. It is bordered by Kansas, Arkansas, Texas, Colorado, New Mexico, and Missouri.

The photograph on the front cover shows rock formations on the plains in Black Kettle National Grassland.

Project Editor: Meredith DeSousa
Art Director: Marie O'Neill
Photo Researcher: Marybeth Kavanagh
Design: Robin West, Ox and Company, Inc.
Page 6 map and recipe art: Susan Hunt Yule
All other maps: XNR Productions, Inc.

Library of Congress Cataloging-in-Publication Data

Saylor-Marchant, Linda.
        Oklahoma / Linda Saylor-Marchant.
          p. cm. – (From sea to shining sea)
        Includes bibliographical references (p.) and index.
        Contents: Introducing the Sooner State—The land of Oklahoma—Oklahoma
through history—Governing Oklahoma—The people and places of Oklahoma—Oklahoma
almanac—Timeline—Gallery of famous Oklahomans.
    ISBN 0-516-22393-3
    1. Oklahoma—Juvenile literature. [1. Oklahoma.] I. Title. II. Series.

F694.3.S295 2003
976.6—dc21   2003000454

TABLE of CONTENTS

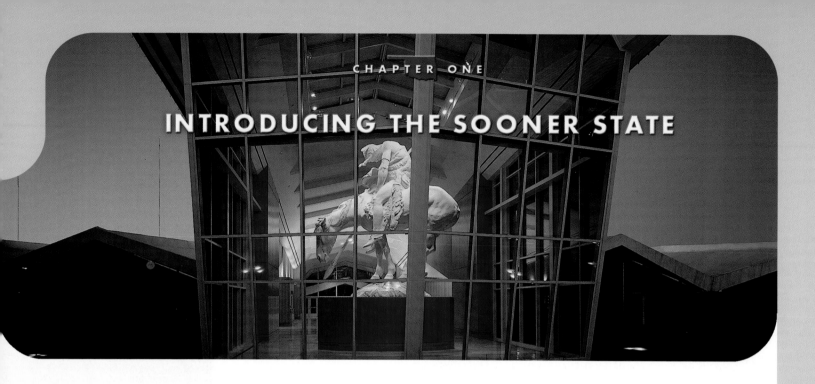

CHAPTER ONE

INTRODUCING THE SOONER STATE

The End of the Trail sculpture, created by James Earle Fraser, is on display at the National Cowboy & Western Heritage Museum in Oklahoma City.

What does Oklahoma mean to you? Does it mean Garth Brooks singing one of his latest hits? Does it mean a colorful Native American powwow? Or maybe a delicious, hot bowl of chili, a favorite dish enjoyed by rugged cowboys of the past? Oklahoma is all this and much more.

The word *Oklahoma* comes from two Choctaw words: *okla,* meaning "people," and *humma,* meaning "red." In the mid-1500s, Native Americans from the Osage, Comanche, Caddo, Wichita, Quapaw, and Ute tribes met European explorers. The visitors explored the land and named territories, bringing a whole new way of life and culture to the native inhabitants of the region. Over time, the United States government declared Oklahoma "Indian Territory" and forced Native Americans from all parts of the country to move there. Today, more than 250,000 Native Americans live in Oklahoma.

Oklahoma got its nickname, the Sooner State, during the late 1880s. In an effort to attract new settlers, the United States government opened the land to anyone who wanted to claim it. On April 22, 1889, the sound of a bugle and numerous gunshots were heard, and crowds of men, women, and children rushed into the area, with a cloud of dust following close behind. This raucous scene became known as the Great Land Run. Anxious settlers who sneaked into the area ahead of time— or too soon—were called Sooners.

What else comes to mind when you think of Oklahoma?

❖ Thousands of Native Americans walking the Trail of Tears to Indian Territory

❖ Pioneers living in soddies on the Oklahoma plains

❖ American Indians gathering in Oklahoma City to celebrate Red Earth, the nation's largest Native American cultural festival

❖ Famous Oklahoma natives, such as actress Countess Vaughn, country music star Reba McEntire, actor Brad Pitt, and opera singer Leona Mitchell

❖ Football fans in Oklahoma Memorial Stadium cheering for the Sooners

❖ Western art and sculptures at the world-renowned National Cowboy & Western Heritage Museum

Oklahoma's story is one of adventure and excitement. Read on to learn more about the history of Oklahoma, Native America, and how dedicated people help make Oklahoma one of the greatest states.

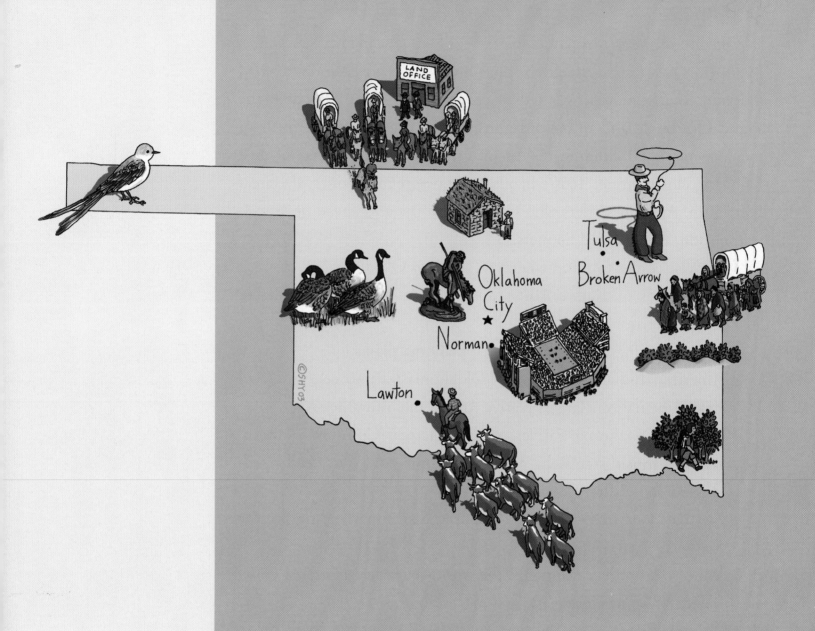

LAND OFFICE

Tulsa

Broken Arrow

Oklahoma City

Norman

Lawton

©SHY03

CHAPTER TWO

THE LAND OF OKLAHOMA

Oklahoma is located in the south central United States. It has an interesting shape. It looks like it has a handle attached to it—like the handle of a pan found in your kitchen. This is why Oklahoma is sometimes referred to as the Panhandle State.

Oklahoma is surrounded by six states. On the northern border you will find Kansas and Colorado. Arkansas and Missouri are to the east, and Texas is to the south and west, along with a small slice of New Mexico on the western border.

Oklahoma ranks eighteenth in size when compared to other states. It covers 69,919 square miles (181,089 square kilometers). This includes the vast inland waters that flow throughout the state. Oklahoma's Panhandle, located in the western part of the state, is just 167 miles (269 kilometers) long and 34 miles (55 km) wide.

The flat landscape in some parts of Oklahoma provides dramatic scenery.

7

The scenic Arbuckle Mountains are in south central Oklahoma.

Much of Oklahoma is flat, but the state is much more than a dusty plain. It has a variety of landscapes that are breathtaking. The rivers, valleys, mountains, and plains are what make this state unique.

MOUNTAIN REGIONS

Oklahoma's mountainous regions include the Arbuckle, Wichita, and Ouachita mountains. The Arbuckle Mountains were once as high as the Himalayas, the highest mountain system in the world, located in Asia. As a result of millions of years of erosion, or wearing away, these mountains now stand only 600 to 700 feet (180 to 210 meters) high. Turner Falls, a popular tourist site, is found there. This land is also used for cattle ranching.

The Wichita Mountain region is located in southwest Oklahoma. In addition to the mountains that cover this area, there are several artificial lakes. There is also a national wildlife preservation site called the Wichita Mountain Wildlife Refuge. In 1905 President Theodore Roosevelt established this site to save the endangered buffalo (also called bison). Hundreds of years ago, these creatures were hunted and killed for food, clothing, and shelter. During the mid-1800s, professional hunters killed bison to prevent them from interfering with the operation of the newly built railroad lines. Other animals found in this area are prairie dogs, birds, elk, and reptiles.

The Ouachita Mountains are located in southeast Oklahoma. These high sandstone ridges run east to west and include the Blue Bouncer, Buffalo, Jackfork, Kiamichi, Rich, and Winding Stair ranges.

FORESTS, PLAINS, AND HILLS

The Sandstone Hills are a heavily forested part of Oklahoma that borders Kansas and extends southward near the Red River region. There are two types of forests there, blackjack and post oak. The Sandstone Hills are covered with sand and rise between 250 and 400 feet (76 and 122 m). Crops such as corn, soybeans, and fruit are grown there. Oil was found in this region during the late 1800s and early 1900s. There are still important oil wells in the area today.

Other regions that share the same characteristics as the Sandstone Hills are the Gypsum Hills, the High Plains, the Ozark Plateau, and the Red Bed Plains. Despite their names, these areas are made up of a variety of colorful landforms.

The Gypsum Hills region has hills that rise from 150 to 200 feet (46 to 61 m). They are covered with gypsum, a soft, white or yellow mineral that sometimes forms transparent or see-through crystals. When the sun hits the top of these hilltops, they sparkle like diamonds.

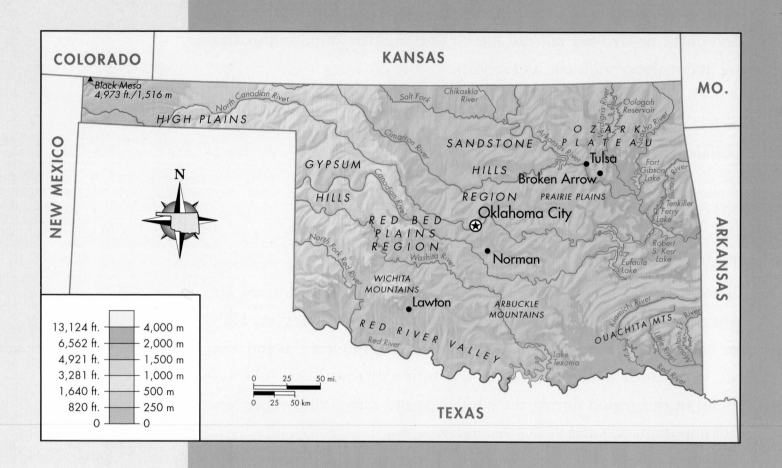

COLORADO

KANSAS

MO.

▲ Black Mesa
4,973 ft./1,516 m

North Canadian River

Salt Fork

Chikaskia River

Oologah Reservoir

HIGH PLAINS

Cimarron River

O Z A R K
P L A T E A U

NEW MEXICO

SANDSTONE

Arkansas River

Verdigris River

Neosho River

● Tulsa

GYPSUM

HILLS

Canadian River

HILLS

Broken Arrow ●

Fort Gibson Lake

Illinois River

REGION

PRAIRIE PLAINS

Tenkiller Ferry Lake

RED BED
PLAINS
REGION

⊛ Oklahoma City

North Fork Red River

Washita River

● Norman

Robert S. Kerr Lake

ARKANSAS

WICHITA
MOUNTAINS

Eufaula Lake

● Lawton

ARBUCKLE
MOUNTAINS

Kiamichi River

OUACHITA MTS.

Mountain Fk. River

R E D   R I V E R   V A L L E Y

Red River

Lake Texoma

Little River

Red River

TEXAS

13,124 ft.	4,000 m
6,562 ft.	2,000 m
4,921 ft.	1,500 m
3,281 ft.	1,000 m
1,640 ft.	500 m
820 ft.	250 m
0	0

0   25   50 mi.

0   25   50 km

The Ozark Plateau is located in the northeast corner of the state. This region is also filled with plenty of hills, swiftly running streams, and steep river valleys.

The Red Bed Plains region is the largest land area of Oklahoma. It has fertile, grassy land areas along with a downward rolling plain that stretches east to west. Two different types of rock are found in this region, shale and sandstone. Shale is a kind of rock that is formed from hardened mud, and sandstone is a type of rock that is formed mostly from sand.

The Prairie Plains area is located west and south of the Ozark Plateau. Farming and cattle ranching take place there. Farmers grow vegetables such as spinach, carrots, and snap beans. Coal and petroleum also come from this region. Many farms are also located in the Red River Plains region in southern Oklahoma. Farmers grow peanuts, cotton, and vegetables in this region's rich and fertile soil.

The High Plains are found in northwest Oklahoma, or the Panhandle. This region is called the High Plains because the land rises as high as 2,000 feet (610 m) on the eastern edge, to 4,973 feet (1,516 m) at Black Mesa—the highest point in Oklahoma. The lowest point in the state is 287 feet (87 m) above sea level, along the Little River in McCurtain County.

Visitors can get a good view of Oklahoma's High Plains region from Black Mesa.

There are 23,000 miles (37,015 km) of rivers and streams in Oklahoma. The Arkansas and Red rivers are two major river systems within the state. The Arkansas River enters the state from Kansas and flows through northeast Oklahoma. Its main tributaries, or branches, are the North and South Canadian rivers and the Cimarron River. The Chikaskia, Grand (Neosho), Poteau, Verdigris, Illinois, and Salt Fork rivers are also important tributaries of the Arkansas River. During the mid- to late 1900s, the Arkansas River became a major part of the Arkansas River Navigational Project. This project was designed to create a large waterway for shipping vessels to pass safely through the state.

The Arkansas River has long been an important means of transportation.

The Red River forms Oklahoma's border with Texas. Its main tributaries are the Blue, Kiamichi, Little, Mountain Fork, and Washita Rivers; Cache Creek; and the North Fork of the Red River.

Oklahoma has more than three hundred beautiful lakes. About two hundred are man-made, and about one hundred are natural. Several of the artificial, or man-made, lakes were built to control flooding and to create hydroelectric plants to generate electricity from water power. Oklahoma's largest lake is Lake Eufaula, located in east-central Oklahoma. Tourists enjoy boating, camping, and fishing at this lake. Other Oklahoma lakes are Tenkiller Ferry Lake, Fort Gibson Lake, and Robert S. Kerr Lake.

PLANTS AND ANIMALS

Oklahoma has an interesting mix of mammals and birds, including armadillos, coyotes, rabbits, prairie dogs, opossums, mink, otters, foxes, squirrels, and black bears. Just about every species of bird found from the Mississippi River Valley to the Rocky Mountains flies in Oklahoma. As you gaze into the sky you may see cardinals, orioles, mockingbirds, meadowlarks, blackbirds, blue jays, robins, and scissor-tailed fly-catchers, Oklahoma's state bird. Scissor-

The scissor-tailed flycatcher has a long, scissorlike tail.

tailed flycatchers, with their stunning, long feathers, are protected in Oklahoma. It is against the law to kill them.

Oklahoma also has lots of trees—more than 133 different varieties. Some trees bear fruit, others bloom, and some are great for shade. Sagebrush is found in the west, and mesquite is found in the southwest. Pine, shortleaf, and various species of elm, oak, ash, hickory, pecan, willow, cypress, and magnolia are found in southern Oklahoma. Juniper and red cedar trees grow abundantly throughout the state and among the canyons of the Gypsum Hills and Red Bed regions.

A portion of the Cross Timbers of Oklahoma are located less than 15 miles (24 km) from Tulsa. These ancient woodlands contain 300- to 500-year-old trees. Their trunks are twisted with age, making the forest impossible to travel through. The forests stretch from Texas to Oklahoma and into Kansas.

EXTRA! EXTRA!

The mesquite tree began spreading through the Southwest during the late 1800s, replacing the grass that cattle feasted on. Cows would eat the mesquite beans and then deposit them wherever they walked. The beans grew into patches of shrubs and trees, and later into forests. Many ranchers and farmers tried to eliminate these annoying shrubs, but it proved to be impossible. Today, some agriculturalists believe that farmers can make money by using the mesquite rather than destroying it. Mesquite beans have the same nutritional value as oats and corn, and wood from mesquite can be used to make fence posts, houses, and fuel. These trees do not need much water to survive.

Oklahoma has a history of unpredictable weather. The dust bowl years, when a severe drought forced thousands of people out of the state in the 1930s, have not been forgotten. During the summer of 1998, Oklahoma farmers were reminded that droughts are not just a thing of the past. Many lost their crops due to lack of rainfall. Even ranchers were affected by the dry weather. Some sold their cattle because there simply wasn't enough green grass around to feed them.

The state also experiences tornadoes. In fact, some of the most violent tornadoes in weather history have occurred in Oklahoma. These violent storms can cause almost anything on the ground to be lifted into

A tornado can easily destroy or damage anything in its path.

the air by winds swirling at record-breaking speeds. Roofs have been blown from the tops of houses, walls have been ripped out, and strong winds have carried cars, trucks, and even buses miles away.

The worst tornadoes reported to date occurred on May 3, 1999, when at least forty tornadoes ripped through central and southwestern Oklahoma. More than 500 people were injured, and 43 people died. The tornadoes also caused more than $35 million worth of damage. Oklahoma averages dozens of tornadoes each year.

At the Severe Storms Laboratory and the Storm Prediction Center, both located in Oklahoma, weather experts called meteorologists work to track down deadly storms before they happen. Thanks to the invention of the Doppler radar system, meteorologists are able to measure the speed and direction of storms before they reach the ground.

There is also a calmer side to Oklahoma's weather. In general, Oklahoma has a relatively mild climate, with hot summers and cold winters. The weather varies in each region. The Panhandle is the coldest, driest, and windiest region of Oklahoma because of its

Residents of Enid make their way through the streets after a winter storm.

elevation, which is the highest in the state. It gets much warmer in Oklahoma's middle to lower regions. The average July temperature is 82° Fahrenheit (28° Celsius). The average January temperature is 37° F (3° C).

Average precipitation ranges from about 50 inches (127 centimeters) per year in the southeast to around 15 inches (38 cm) in the western Panhandle. Snowfall ranges from up to 2 inches (5 cm) in the southeast to 25 inches (64 cm) in the northwest. The heaviest snow falls in the Panhandle.

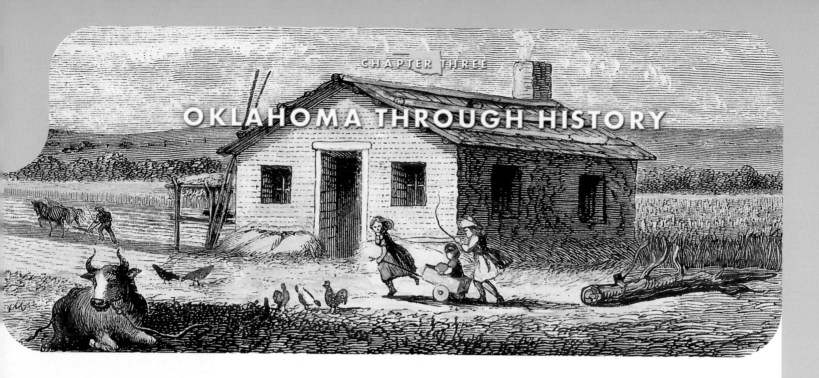

CHAPTER THREE

OKLAHOMA THROUGH HISTORY

Many homesteaders lived in sod huts on the western prairie.

People roamed the land we now call Oklahoma as far back as 15,000 years ago. They were not alone. Their company included prehistoric creatures that were hunted for food, shelter, and clothing. Today, archaeologists have uncovered artifacts of prehistoric life in various parts of Oklahoma. These artifacts include primitive homes and wall inscriptions. They have also found dinosaur bones and footprints that are millions of years old.

The earliest inhabitants of Oklahoma were the Clovis people. On a typical day, a Clovis man would make weapons or spears that would be used for hunting animals. Archaeologists have uncovered the bones of a huge mammoth—a large mammal, now extinct, that is related to the modern-day elephant—and several spear points near Anadarko. Research findings indicate that these spear points belonged to the Clovis hunters.

Other prehistoric groups that followed the Clovis were the Plainview, Folsom, and Mound Builders. From A.D. 500 to 1300, the Mound Builders inhabited the area west of the Arkansas-Oklahoma border in LeFlore County. They built large earth mounds, or burial sites, that resembled flat-topped pyramids. Some of these mounds can be seen today at Spiro Mounds Archaeological Park. Archaeologists have found artifacts such as copper plaques, conch shells, and religious ceremonial items inside the Spiro Mounds.

The Spiro Mounds contain evidence of an early culture that once lived in Oklahoma.

EARLY NATIVE AMERICANS

Some of the early Native American tribes living in Oklahoma at the beginning of the historic period were the Caddo, Wichita, Quapaw, Osage, Comanche, and Ute. The Caddo, who lived along the Red River, and the Wichita, from the southwest, claim to be the oldest inhabitants of the state. Their homes were made of thatched grass. The Osage and Quapaw lived in homes that were covered with bark and sometimes buffalo skins. They lived in small villages, planting corn and hunting buffalo. The Comanche and the Ute stayed in the mountains and hills. Their homes were similar to those of the Osage and Quapaw. They did not plant crops or cultivate the soil. Instead, they traded with people from other tribes for corn. They also gathered roots, fruits, and herbs, and hunted buffalo for food. These tribes, with the exception of the Ute, are still living in the state today.

After a while, other tribes, such as the Kiowa, Delaware, Shawnee, and Kickapoo, lived in different parts of the region. These tribes were called Plains Indians.

THE AGE OF EXPLORATION

In the year 1012 brave Norsemen called Vikings sailed their ships against the raging waters of the Atlantic Ocean. One tale tells of a Viking ship that sailed around Florida to the Gulf of Mexico, up the Mississippi River, and all the way to the Arkansas and Poteau rivers. Not far away, a huge block of sandstone was found on Poteau Mountain in

The Heavener Runestone remains one of Oklahoma's great mysteries.

Heavener. An eight-character inscription called a rune was carved into the stone. Some people believe that the inscription represents a date—November 11, 1012—carved by the Vikings. Similar inscriptions were found on two stones nearby.

More than four centuries later, European explorers from Spain and France began to arrive in Oklahoma. In 1541, Spanish explorers, called conquistadores, were the first Europeans to set foot in Oklahoma. Francisco Vásquez de Coronado came from Mexico in search of the Seven Cities of Gold. No explorer knew the exact location of these cities, but each hoped to find them during his expeditions.

Coronado's group explored much of the Southwest.

When Coronado arrived in what is now called Oklahoma, he had with him a large group of Spanish soldiers and Native Americans. A Plains Indian told him stories about a rich city called Quivira, where gold bells hung from the trees and women poured drinks from golden pitchers. However, when Coronado and his men reached Quivira, located in Kansas near modern-day Oklahoma, they saw only primitive villages. After seeing that there was no gold, Coronado blamed his guide and had him killed.

Hernando de Soto, another Spanish explorer, may have arrived in Oklahoma in 1542. Like Coronado, he was looking for gold. De Soto, who was also the first European to see the Mississippi River, died of a fever on the banks of the river that same year.

More Europeans arrived in Oklahoma in 1673. Unlike the Spanish explorers who were seeking gold, French explorers were interested in fur.

While on Oklahoma soil the French established a fur trading business with Native Americans, who were skilled at hunting and trapping beavers and other fur-bearing animals. Furs traded in the region were shipped to Europe to make fashionable clothing, including hats, hand-warmers, and shakos, which are tall military hats with plumes.

To get as much fur as possible, the French set up trading posts all along Oklahoma's rivers. Trading posts along the Neosho, Verdigris, and Canadian rivers were well stocked with European and Asian goods such as vermilion (red dye that comes from the mineral cinnabar), silver, knives, beads, awls, sugar, mirrors, copper kettles, cloth, horse tack, clothing, guns, and ammunition. These goods were traded in exchange for beaver, otter, bear, raccoon, buffalo, and bobcat pelts.

Native Americans were skilled hunters and often traded furs with Europeans.

La Salle claimed the Mississippi River Valley for France.

EXTRA! EXTRA!

The members of the Chouteau family were French explorers who settled in New Orleans, Louisiana. They owned a lucrative fur trading business in the area. The trade partners consisted of two half brothers—Renè Auguste and Jean Pierre; and Jean Pierre's sons, Auguste and Pierre. Together they set up several trading posts along Oklahoma's rivers, including posts on the Missouri River and in the Three Forks region of the Arkansas River—the Neosho, Verdigris, and Canadian rivers. They also founded Salina, one of the first permanent European settlements in Oklahoma.

In 1682 another French explorer, René-Robert Cavelier, Sieur de La Salle, led an expedition down the Mississippi River to the Gulf of Mexico. He claimed all the land touching the Mississippi River for France and named it Louisiana, in honor of the French king, Louis XIV. Other French explorers and traders who traveled in and around Oklahoma were Louis Jolliet, Jacques Marquette, Louis Juchereau de St. Denis, Bernard de la Harpe, and the Chouteaus. By 1819, French fur traders had established the first European settlements in Salina and Three Forks.

THE LOUISIANA PURCHASE

By the beginning of the 1800s, the United States owned all the land east of the Mississippi River. Although much of the land west of the river belonged to France, United States President Thomas Jefferson became interested in staking a claim to it. Acquiring this territory meant creating a bigger, stronger United States.

In 1803 France decided to sell the Louisiana Territory to the United States for just $15 million. The territory covered more than 800,000 square miles (2 million sq km)—including much of present-day Oklahoma—and nearly doubled the size of the United States. This historic

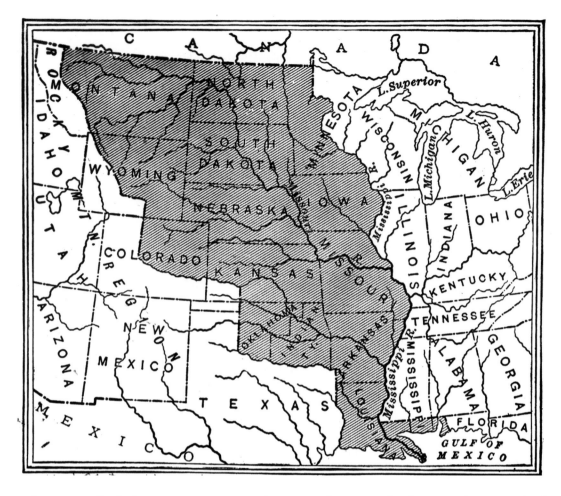

The Louisiana Purchase, shown in gray, included a large part of today's Midwest.

sale was called the Louisiana Purchase, and it was the best real estate deal in our nation's history.

President Thomas Jefferson hired explorers to locate boundary lines and establish forts to protect the new territory. The expedition was headed by Meriwether Lewis and William Clark. Lewis and Clark explored the upper part of the Louisiana Territory. The lower part of the territory, where present-day Oklahoma is located, was explored by Captain Richard Sparks, Captain Zebulon Pike, Lieutenant James Wilkinson, and George Sibley. These brave and courageous explorers had interesting and exciting stories to tell when they returned from their expeditions.

Captain Richard Sparks explored the lower Louisiana Territory. His team traveled the Red River north and west to its very beginning. As soon as they reached the southwestern corner of the Louisiana Territory, however, they were turned away by angry Spanish soldiers guarding the Panhandle, which still belonged to Spain.

Zebulon Pike's exploratory team reached Belle Point on the eastern border of Oklahoma in 1807. George Sibley and his men stumbled on the valuable salt deposits in the Great Salt Plains region. In 1819 Major Steven Long found the source of the Arkansas River in the Rocky Mountains and one of its tributaries, the Canadian River. He then established Fort Smith along the Oklahoma-Arkansas border.

Thomas Nuttall, a botanist, led a scientific expedition through the territory. During his journey he collected information about Oklahoma's rocks, minerals, plants, and animals. This valuable information was published in *A Journal of Travels Into the Arkansas Territory*.

INDIAN TERRITORY

By the early 1800s, the eastern United States was bursting at the seams with European and American settlers. These settlers wanted land, and this often meant taking Native American land. As more settlers arrived in the southeastern United States—Georgia, the Carolinas, Florida, and Mississippi—they took over the land by force, sometimes violently raiding Native American villages. Other settlers pressured the United States government to move the Native Americans elsewhere.

In 1804 the settlers got what they wanted. Congress passed a law that gave the president power to order Native Americans off their tribal lands onto "Unassigned Lands," or what was called Indian Territory. This territory included present-day Oklahoma, and it was intended only for Native Americans.

The United States government asked Native Americans to sign a removal treaty, or agreement. Some signed the treaty, but others protested. Some of the protesters fought against the government in what became known as the Indian Wars. Others, who resisted by refusing to sign the treaty, watched as United States agents burned their homes to the ground.

In 1838, the United States government began the removal of American Indians to Oklahoma. The first tribes to be removed from the Southeast were known as the Five Civilized Tribes: the Cherokee, the Choctaw, the Creek, the Seminole, and the Chickasaw. Europeans referred to them as "civilized" because they dressed and acted like Europeans. For example, they had their own schools, businesses, plantations, and slaves.

That year, 15,000 Native American men, women, and children began a long and difficult journey westward to Indian Territory. When winter approached, they had not yet reached their destination. Through the miserable cold, they pressed on. Thousands died as a result of freezing temperatures, starvation, and deadly diseases. This brutal journey became known as the Trail of Tears.

Nearly one-fifth of the Cherokee population died on the Trail of Tears.

As soon as the Five Civilized Tribes arrived on their new land, they worked hard to reestablish themselves. The United States government had assured them that this land now belonged to them, as long as "the grass shall grow and rivers run." Within a short period of time they built homes, businesses, and plantations. Each tribe organized its own government, elected leaders, and established its own schools and churches. Both the Cherokee and the Choctaw created their own advanced educational systems. It was there that Sequoyah, inventor of the Cherokee alphabet, taught many of his people how to read and write. The Cherokee published Oklahoma's first Native American newspaper in Indian Territory, the *Cherokee Phoenix,* in 1828, and the first Cherokee newspaper printed in both English and Cherokee, the *Cherokee Advocate,* in 1844.

THE CIVIL WAR

By the mid-1800s, another conflict had developed within the United States. This time it was between the Northern and Southern states. At that time, the South depended mainly on agriculture (farming) to make money. Southern landowners owned massive farms, or plantations, that needed many workers. Often, slaves were used. Slaves were Africans who were kidnapped from their native lands and brought to the United States, where they were bought and sold among landowners. Slaves were forced to perform backbreaking work without pay, and they were beaten or even killed if they tried to escape. Through the use of slaves, plantations were able to produce massive amounts of cotton, a crop that brought in much money to the South. In contrast, the Northern economy was based on both farming and manufacturing, where workers were employed for pay. In fact, slavery was illegal in many Northern states.

As new states joined the Union, arguments erupted as to whether they should be slave states or free states (states without slavery). When Abraham Lincoln was elected president of the United States in 1860, many Southerners worried that he would try to put an end to slavery. They believed that each state should be able to make its own decisions. In protest, many Southern states voted to withdraw from the Union. Together, they formed a new nation called the Confederate States of America.

In 1861 the Civil War (1861–1865) broke out. The Southern states formed the Confederate, or Rebel, army. The army of the Northern

The Battle of Pea Ridge took place just outside Indian Territory in 1862.

states was called the Union army. Both sides recruited soldiers from the West to fight in the war. When the armies reached Indian Territory, which was neutral, some Native Americans agreed to fight on the side of the Union. Others, who were still angry at the United States for taking their land, joined the Confederate army.

No major battles took place in or around Indian Territory. However, several bloody skirmishes were fought in the area, including the Battles of Pea Ridge, Locust Grove, and Honey Springs. During the Battle of Cabin Creek, Brigadier General Stand Watie, a Native American Confederate leader, and his troops captured 300 Union wagons loaded with supplies. Watie and his troops fought until the bitter end. He finally gave up at Fort Towson in 1865, making him

EXTRA! EXTRA!

African-American soldiers who were once farmers, cowboys, and gunfighters fought alongside the Union army in the Civil War. After the war ended, African-Americans became part of the 9th and 10th Cavalry units. These units were established by Congress, and their headquarters were located at Fort Sill and Fort Gibson. While working at the forts, these soldiers had numerous responsibilities, which included fighting off thieves and bandits. They were nicknamed the Buffalo Soldiers by Native Americans for their fierce fighting skills.

the last Confederate leader in his territory to surrender. The Civil War ended in 1865, when Confederate general Robert E. Lee surrendered to Union general Ulysses S. Grant.

AFTER THE WAR

Native Americans in Indian Territory suffered tremendously after the war. Their homes and property were destroyed. Those who had joined the Confederate army were punished. They were stripped of their land and moved into smaller tracts of land in the Eastern Territory, or eastern Oklahoma.

Native Americans from the Great Plains, called Plains Indians, were forced to live on reservations. These Plains Indians were descendants of the native tribes that had occupied the Red River region during European exploration. This second Indian removal became known as the Second Trail of Tears.

The lands that were vacated would soon be occupied by thousands of white settlers. In 1862 Congress passed the Homestead Act. This act provided 160 acres (65 hectares) of free land to any citizen who would live on and cultivate it for a period of five years. As a result, many people

Thousands of settlers traveled west in oxen-drawn wagons, hoping to acquire land.

migrated to the Great Plains, including parts of Oklahoma.

COWBOYS AND CATTLE DRIVES

After the war there was a strong demand for beef in the north and east. At the time, there were great numbers of longhorn cattle in Texas. To take advantage of this new demand, ranchers began hiring cowboys to herd the cattle from Texas to northern towns, where they could be shipped north and east. Cowboys blazed new trails to busy Kansas trading towns, such as Abilene, Dodge City, and Wichita.

The legend of the American cowboy grew out of the cattle drive days.

The very first trail that ran through Oklahoma from the Red River to the Arkansas River into Missouri was called the East Shawnee Trail. This trail followed a route known as the Texas Road, and settlers and merchants traveled this route for many years. Today, the Texas Road is Highway 69 and the Missouri-Kansas-Texas Railroad. The trail that ran through west central Oklahoma, linking Texas with Kansas, was called the Chisholm Trail. Another well-known trail was the West Shawnee Trail, which led to Dodge City. The Jones-Plummer Trail, which crossed Oklahoma's Panhandle, was used by cowboys heading westward.

From 1866 to 1889, more than six million longhorn cattle crossed trails on Native American lands. During this time, several cattle ranchers established business relationships with Native Americans. In 1883 a group of cattle ranchers leased more than 6 million acres (2.4 million ha) of land from Native Americans for five years. Some ranchers paid for the use of the lands, and others didn't. This business soon came to a halt in 1890, when all leases were declared invalid because they were not authorized by the United States government. American citizens were now barred from settling on or conducting business on these lands. President Benjamin Harrison immediately ordered all cattle belonging to white ranchers removed.

RODEOS AND WILD WEST SHOWS

The end of the cattle-driving days did not stop ranch owners and cowboys from making money. Many people enjoyed watching the cowboys work, and it wasn't long before cowboys were showing off their riding and roping skills to crowds of people. Cowboys represented the

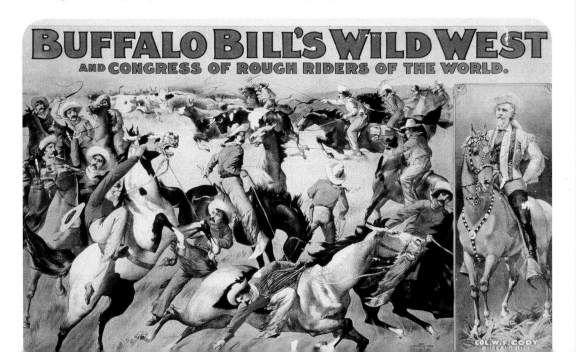

Advertisements such as these drew large crowds to Wild West shows.

"Wild West," and people from all over the country wanted to get in on the excitement. Some cowboys began touring the country, fascinating audiences with longhorn steers, bucking broncos, and roundups. These tours were called Wild West shows. Pawnee Bill, Buffalo Bill, and the Miller Brothers 101 Ranch Wild West Show were some of the most popular.

THE GREAT LAND RUNS

After 1866, a large portion of Indian Territory was unoccupied. It became known as the Unassigned Lands. It didn't take long for word to get out about the large land area that was open and available for settlement. "Boomers," or professional land promoters, were hired to help spread the word and convince homesteaders, railroad companies, families, and farm businesses to move into this new territory. Two well-known boomers were David L. Payne and William Couch. They were responsible for lining up thousands of anxious homesteaders along Oklahoma's borders before the Unassigned Lands were officially opened.

In March 1889, President Benjamin Harrison announced a date for the official opening of the Unassigned Lands—April 22, 1889. On this day at noon, more than 2 million acres (800,000 ha) of the Unassigned Lands would be open to the public. Citizens who were interested in claiming land were to follow the homestead laws—cultivate and live on the land for five years, after which 160 acres (65 ha) would be granted.

Hopeful crowds gathered at the border of the Unassigned Lands in preparation for a land run.

More than 50,000 people gathered at the border and waited for the sound of the pistol so they could rush in and make their claim. There were some who could not wait, and they managed to sneak in before the land was officially open. Some were caught by federal troops, and others got away with it. These people were called Sooners. To make it look as if they arrived when everyone else did, Sooners raced their horses around until they were out of breath.

When the shot rang out, the settlers ran as fast as they could to get their land. Some were on foot, and others arrived in covered wagons. It was a mad rush because there was not enough land for

Guthrie began to look like a small town just five days after the land was opened to settlers in 1889.

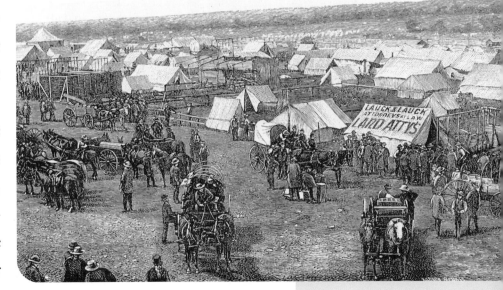

everyone. Within a single night, two cities were born: Oklahoma City, with 10,000 people, and Guthrie, with more than 15,000. Another land rush took place on September 16, 1893, at the Cherokee Outlet—the biggest land rush in history. On this day more than 100,000 people rushed in to claim land.

NEW TERRITORY, NEW NAME

In 1890 Congress established a divided Oklahoma—Oklahoma Territory and Indian Territory. Oklahoma Territory had 78,000 people and was located west of Indian Territory. Indian Territory had 180,000 people. Twin Territories was the new name given to the divided region.

After the land runs, more Native American land was purchased by the United States government. Indian Territory began to shrink. Under the leadership of President Benjamin Harrison, the United States government appointed two special commissions. The Dawes and Jerome commissions were created to encourage Native Americans to give up their lands and move to smaller tracts of land called reservations. While living on reservations, the tribes would be prepared for American citizenship. On the reservations, there would be schools, recreational facilities, churches, and stores.

Decisions made by both commissions reduced Native American lands tremendously. Native Americans spoke out against the decisions. Kiowa leader Lone Wolf went to the Supreme Court and appealed the decisions made by the Jerome Commission. Wolf's case stated that these new changes violated earlier treaties the government had made with his tribe. However, his appeal was denied, and the Supreme Court declared that Congress had the right to abolish, or do away with, the provisions of an Indian treaty.

BLACK GOLD

Land was not the only valuable resource in the Twin Territories during the late 1800s. There was something else that helped to improve Oklahoma's economy—oil, or "black gold." In 1889 oil prospector Edward Byrd spent several days drilling for oil and found what he was looking for in Chelsea. Another successful oil prospector was Frank Phillips.

Soon after the discovery of oil in Oklahoma, prospectors invaded the territory in search of more "black gold."

Phillips drilled the first commercial oil well in Bartlesville in 1897 and founded the Phillips Petroleum Company in 1917.

The oil discoveries in Oklahoma were very timely. In 1896 a man named Henry Ford began to develop the automobile, which needed oil to run. With thousands of people purchasing automobiles across the country, there was now a strong demand for oil. The Twin Territories began to export huge amounts of oil to wherever it was needed.

Oil fields were also discovered in Tulsa. The Red Fork oil field was discovered in 1901. Four years later, in 1905, the Glenpool oil field was discovered. As a result of these discoveries, Tulsa became known as the Oil Capital of the World. Other oil towns were Bartlesville, Ponca City, Ardmore, Seminole, Tonkawa, Cushing, Avant, and Okmulgee.

Record-breaking amounts of oil gushed from wells in Oklahoma City during the early 1900s. In 1928 one well sprayed about 6,500 barrels of oil in one day, and just fifteen months later another well, called "Wild Mary Sudik," spewed oil for eleven days straight. It was estimated that this well splattered 20,000 barrels each day, splashing everything around it, including livestock and homes. Finally, on April 6, 1930, a team of brave engineers capped the well and stopped it from flowing.

STATEHOOD

In 1905 the leaders of the Five Civilized Tribes called a constitutional convention in Muskogee. These tribes wanted to form their own state. They adopted a constitution for a proposed state to be named in honor of Sequoyah, the Cherokee leader. They also held an election, and the members who attended the convention voted and approved of this new state. The election results were brought to Congress and the Dawes Commission. Congress, in favor of forming one state, not two, refused to acknowledge Sequoyah as a state.

On November 16, 1907, President Theodore Roosevelt signed the official statehood proclamation, and Oklahoma became a state. Oklahoma was the forty-sixth state to enter the Union, with a population of 1,414,177. The Sooner State's first capital was Guthrie, and in 1910 Oklahoma City became the state's permanent capital.

WHAT'S IN A NAME?

Many names of places in Oklahoma have interesting origins.

Name	Comes From or Means
Tishomingo	Named for a warrior king of the Chickasaw tribe who died on the journey to Indian Territory
Black Wall Street	Nickname given to Greenwood, a prosperous African-American neighborhood located in Tulsa
Okmulgee	Creek word meaning "bubbling water"
Norman	Named for Abner E. Norman, a surveyor who worked during the 1870s
No Man's Land	Strip of Cherokee land between Kansas and Texas belonging to no territory or state from 1850 to 1890; it later became known as the Oklahoma Panhandle

Sequoyah created the Cherokee alphabet.

RACIAL TENSION

Although many African-Americans had hoped to find their promised land in Oklahoma, there were still problems to overcome. Since the late

A group of injured rioters are taken to the hospital by National Guardsmen after the race riot of 1921.

1800s, segregation laws were in effect in Oklahoma and many other states across the South. These laws separated blacks from whites. Under these "Jim Crow" laws, African-Americans were required to sit at the back of buses and trains, use special entrances to enter and exit public facilities, use "colored" rest rooms and water fountains, and were forbidden to marry whites.

There were also other forms of hatred directed at African-Americans. One was the emergence of the Ku Klux Klan, a hate group that terrorized many African-Americans. This group was responsible for destroying a prosperous African-American neighborhood in the Greenwood section of Tulsa known as Black Wall Street. It was given this name because more than 11,000 wealthy African-Americans lived and operated businesses within the town's thirty-five blocks. In 1921, thousands of angry whites flooded the streets, destroying property and breaking into stores. Churches were burned to the ground, and there were reports of up to 300 deaths. It was considered one of the worst race riots in America's history. After a decade of rebuilding, Greenwood became a viable neighborhood once again and was even more prosperous than before.

The racial climate changed in the 1950s and 1960s. In 1954 the Supreme Court ruled that it was unconstitutional for a state to have separate schools for white and black students. This ruling marked the beginning of the Civil Rights movement and the end of the Jim Crow laws.

WORLD WAR I

World War I (1914–1918) broke out in the early 1900s. During the war, the United States government purchased wheat from Oklahoma farmers to help feed United States troops fighting in Europe. This helped Oklahoma's farm economy tremendously. The war brought on a demand for agricultural products, and as a result, some Oklahoma farmers became prosperous.

Oklahoma's economy was stable for a number of years after the war. However, this changed in 1929, when the stock market crashed. This was the beginning of a difficult financial period called the Great Depression, when people living in Oklahoma and in other parts of the United States lost their jobs and homes. Banks failed, prices dropped, factories closed, and thousands of people waited on breadlines to get their daily meals. Oklahoma's chief products, oil, wheat, and cattle, were no

The Great Depression left many families across the country homeless.

longer in demand. Many people became depressed during these hard times and even took their lives.

Things only got worse. Bad weather in the form of dust storms forced thousands of Oklahomans to migrate to California. The dust storms were the result of drought and farmers misusing the land. To keep the dust out of their homes, people stuffed wet rags between the cracks of their windows and doors. Many people and livestock suffered from lung damage caused by breathing in dust. Crops, homes, and other property were destroyed. This period in the history of Oklahoma and other Great Plains states was known as the dust bowl years. Others refer to this period as the "Dirty Thirties."

Two women use handkerchiefs to fight swirling dust and wind in Alva.

PROSPERITY PREVAILS

The Great Depression gradually came to an end at the start of World War II (1939–1945). The war brought forth a demand for many goods and services that Oklahoma could provide. Coal, fuel, and agricultural products were purchased from Oklahoma and sent to soldiers and their families. Two of the state's forts, Fort Sill and Fort Lawton, were busy training soldiers. Two major public works projects—the Turner Turnpike, which connected Oklahoma City and Tulsa; and the McClellan-Kerr Arkansas River Navigation System, which gave the state a powerful source of hydroelectric power, or waterpower—created jobs and a stronger economy for the state.

The McClellan-Kerr Arkansas River Navigation System was completed in 1970. It linked Oklahoma and Arkansas to major ports around the world. As a result, the shipping industry became important to the economy of the state. The navigation system also provided drinking water.

The petroleum (oil) and natural gas industries provided many jobs during the 1970s. Oklahomans have long depended on their state's supply of oil and natural gas to keep their homes, businesses, vehicles, and other machinery running. Other states have also benefited from these resources. However, when the price of oil dropped during the early 1980s, state leaders tried to attract other industries, such as manufacturing, to help balance the state's economy. Supplies and equipment made in Oklahoma include computers, cars, electronics, and aviation and aerospace parts.

TERRORISM

In 1995 one of the worst terrorist acts in the history of the United States occurred in Oklahoma. On April 19 a terrorist bomb blew up Oklahoma

An American flag and memorial flowers were placed at the scene of the Murrah Building shortly after the bombing.

City's Murrah Federal Building. What began as a typical day turned to disaster shortly after 9:00 A.M., when a bomb exploded, tearing the building to shreds. More than 150 people died that day.

Shortly after the explosion, twenty-seven-year-old Timothy McVeigh was pulled over by an Oklahoma Highway Patrol officer for driving without a license plate. Before he was released for this traffic violation, he was identified as a suspect and charged in the bombing. Two years later a jury in Denver convicted McVeigh of this crime and sentenced him to death.

On September 11, 2001, Oklahomans were reminded of their tragedy when terrorists attacked the World Trade Center in New York City and the Pentagon in Washington, D.C. Kari Watkins, executive director of the Oklahoma City National Memorial, said, "We went through a similar tragedy, but ours was on a smaller scale. Oklahomans will offer any help we can because we have been through this before."

To help victims of terrorism, President Bush signed legislation in January of 2002 called the Victims of Terrorism Tax Relief Act. Families of the victims of September 11, the Oklahoma City bombing, and the recent anthrax attacks were not charged income tax for the year of the attack and the previous year. Families of each victim will be provided with a minimum benefit of $10,000.

On a positive note, Oklahoma is building a new economy in the twenty-first century. During this "Information Age," communications technology—including devices such as the Internet, E-mail, DVDs, and cell phones—has advanced greatly. Oklahoma has much to offer technology companies and employees, such as a low cost of living and wide-open spaces. As a result, many people with diverse technological backgrounds working in communications technology have moved to Oklahoma, and high-tech companies have made the Sooner State their home. As the new century continues, Oklahoma may look forward to experiencing a new kind of "land run."

Where the Murrah Building once stood, the Oklahoma City National Memorial now honors the victims, survivors, and rescuers involved in the tragedy.

CHAPTER FOUR

GOVERNING OKLAHOMA

The Oklahoma state capitol was completed in 1917.

Oklahoma is governed according to rules set down in its state constitution. The constitution is an official document that outlines the rights and responsibilities of state government officials and the citizens of Oklahoma. Oklahoma's state constitution was adopted in 1907, the same year the state entered the Union. Many amendments, or changes, have been made to the constitution since its adoption in 1907. Like the United States, Oklahoma has three branches, or parts, of government: the legislative branch, the executive branch, and the judicial branch.

LEGISLATIVE BRANCH

The legislative branch makes the laws of the state. Oklahoma has some very interesting laws. For example, it is against the law to make ugly faces at a dog or to get a fish drunk! A recent law, passed in August

2002, requires all Oklahoma public schools to observe a minute of silence each day for meditation, prayer, or another silent activity.

The legislative branch has two parts: a senate and a house of representatives. The senate has 48 senators and the house of representatives has 101 representatives. Senators and representatives meet from February to May every year. Senators serve four-year terms, while members of the house of representatives serve for just two years.

Any member of the senate or house of representatives may introduce a bill, which is a draft of a proposed new law. The bill must be passed by both the house and the senate and signed by the governor before it becomes law.

EXECUTIVE BRANCH

The executive branch carries out the laws of the state. The governor is the head of the executive branch. He or she is responsible for appointing other members of the executive branch, such as the secretary of state, the secretary of finance, and several state commissioners. The governor serves for a term of four years.

JUDICIAL BRANCH

The third branch of government is the judicial branch. Members of the judicial branch interpret, or explain, the laws of the state. These responsibilities are carried out through the court system.

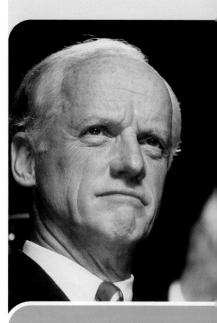

WHO'S WHO IN OKLAHOMA?

Frank Keating (1944–) was first elected to serve as Oklahoma's governor in 1994. He was reelected in 1998. After the bombing of the Murrah Federal Building in Oklahoma City in 1995, Keating supervised the search for survivors and comforted victims and their families. Keating's wife, Cathy, helped raise $7 million for the victims' loved ones. Keating was born in St. Louis, Missouri, and grew up in Tulsa.

OKLAHOMA GOVERNORS

Name	Term	Name	Term
Charles N. Haskell	1907–1911	Johnston Murray	1951–1955
Lee Cruce	1911–1915	Raymond D. Gary	1955–1959
R. L. Williams	1915–1919	J. Howard Edmondson	1959–1963
James B.A. Robertson	1919–1923	George Nigh	1963
John C. Walton	1923	Henry Bellmon	1963–1967
Martin E. Trapp	1923–1927	Dewey F. Bartlett	1967–1971
Henry S. Johnston	1927–1929	David Hall	1971–1975
William J. Holloway	1929–1931	David L. Boren	1975–1979
William H. Murray	1931–1935	George Nigh	1979–1987
Ernest W. Marland	1935–1939	Henry Bellmon	1987–1991
Leon C. Phillips	1939–1943	David Walters	1991–1995
Robert S. Kerr	1943–1947	Frank Keating	1995–2003
Roy J. Turner	1947–1951	Brad Henry	2003–

OKLAHOMA STATE GOVERNMENT

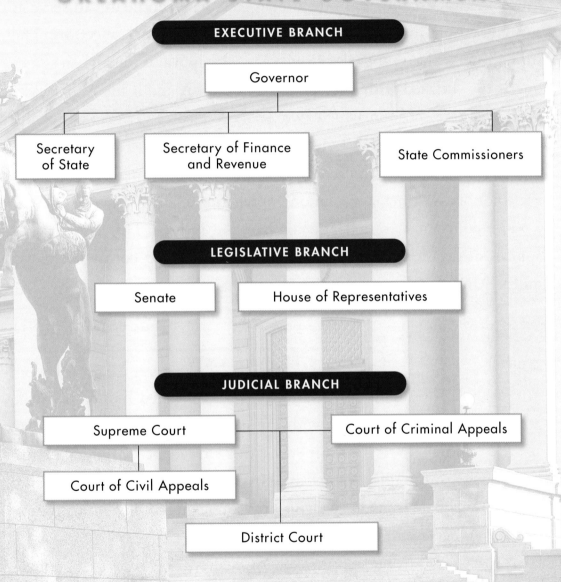

EXECUTIVE BRANCH

Governor

Secretary of State

Secretary of Finance and Revenue

State Commissioners

LEGISLATIVE BRANCH

Senate

House of Representatives

JUDICIAL BRANCH

Supreme Court

Court of Criminal Appeals

Court of Civil Appeals

District Court

Nine justices, or judges, serve on the state supreme court. A group called the nominating commission suggests new candidates to serve as supreme court justices; the governor makes the final selection. The supreme court hears appeals of civil cases. An appeal is filed when someone is not satisfied with a lower court's decision about his or her case. Civil cases are those in which two or more parties disagree about the meaning of a law. These types of cases might involve child custody, divorce, and racial discrimination (treating someone unfairly because of the color of his or her skin), among other things.

The court of criminal appeals has five judges. This court hears appeals of decisions in criminal cases made by lower courts. Robbery, murder, and assault are examples of criminal matters.

Many Native American tribes are headquartered in Oklahoma and are an important part of the state's culture.

TRIBAL LAW

Native Americans have their own laws called Indian, or tribal law. These laws deal with the status of Native American tribes and their relationship with the United States government. There are thirty-nine tribal governments in Oklahoma. Thirty-eight are federally recognized as sovereign nations, which means they have the power to govern themselves.

Census figures reveal that Oklahoma is home to a population of more than 380,000 tribal members. The Cherokee Nation, located in Tahlequah, is the second largest tribe in the United States, with more than 222,000 members. Oklahoma's smallest tribe is the Modoc tribe, with 200 members. Because Oklahoma has such a large Native American population, a state government agency called the Oklahoma Indian Affairs Commission was created to assist Native American individuals and families. It is headquartered in Oklahoma City. The Bureau of Indian Affairs, a United States government agency, also has offices at Muskogee and at Anadarko.

TAKE A TOUR OF OKLAHOMA CITY, THE STATE CAPITAL

Oklahoma City is the state capital. The city has many historic buildings and landmarks that were constructed around the time of statehood. The city's first skyscraper, the Pioneer Telephone Building, was built in the early 1900s. There is also the Carnegie Library, built in 1900 with a donation of $25,000 from Andrew Carnegie. An African-American landmark building is Calvary Baptist Church, built in 1922. Dr. Martin Luther King, Jr. once interviewed for a position as pastor of this church.

To learn more about state government or see state representatives in action, people can visit the state capitol building. When they arrive at the capitol, they will see fourteen flags flying

About one-third of the state's population lives in or near Oklahoma City.

51

A new stained-glass skylight containing the state seal decorates the capitol dome.

high. These flags identify the foreign countries that claimed Oklahoma territory at one time or another throughout history, as well as the current state and United States flags.

Inside the capitol, visitors can look up into the new dome at the state seal decoration, unveiled in July 2002. The seal is made of more than 9,000 bits and pieces of stained glass sealed together by more than a mile of lead. The seal looks like a diamond with fluorescent lights shining through the blue, white, and gold background. This seal replaced the old plaster seal that hung in the state capitol for eighty years.

Aside from the capitol, there are lots of things to see and do in Oklahoma City. You can visit Frontier City Theme Park and ride some of the most exciting rides in the Southwest. Oklahoma City is also home to the Softball Hall of Fame, where you can learn about softball's greatest athletes and their accomplishments.

One of the city's most popular attractions is the National Cowboy and Western Heritage Museum. The museum's art, sculptures, and exhibits tell the story of the Old West, when cowboys rode lonely trails and mountain men roamed the hills. The Hall of Great Westerners honors the many men and women who represent the heart and spirit of the United States' western heritage, including trapper Jim Bridger, novelist Willa Cather, and showman "Buffalo Bill" Cody. You can even visit Prosperity Junction, a re-created town from the early 1900s that includes a blacksmith's shop, a railroad depot, a school, and homes.

When it's time to grab a bite to eat, head for Bricktown, the heart of Oklahoma's entertainment district. Surrounded by restored red-brick

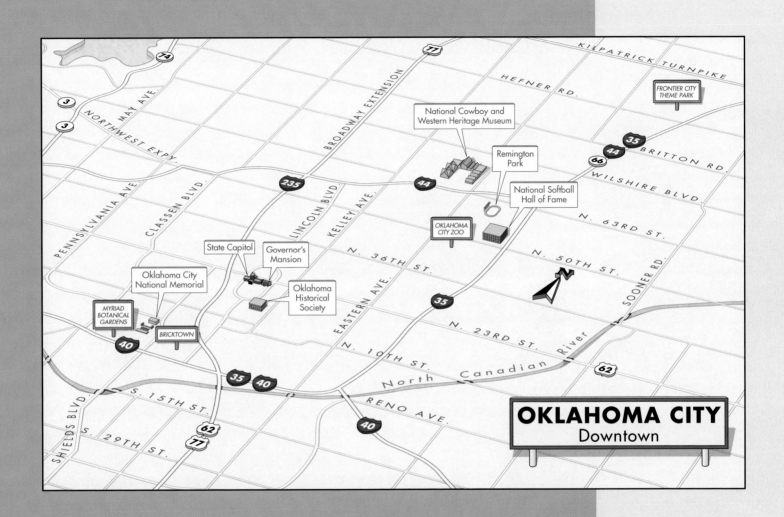

National Cowboy and
Western Heritage Museum

Remington
Park

National Softball
Hall of Fame

OKLAHOMA
CITY ZOO

State Capitol

Governor's
Mansion

Oklahoma City
National Memorial

Oklahoma
Historical
Society

MYRIAD
BOTANICAL
GARDENS

BRICKTOWN

FRONTIER CITY
THEME PARK

KILPATRICK TURNPIKE

HEFNER RD.

BRITTON RD.

WILSHIRE BLVD.

N. 63RD ST.

N. 50TH ST.

SOONER RD.

N. 36TH ST.

N. 23RD ST.

N. 10TH ST.

EASTERN AVE.

KELLEY AVE.

LINCOLN BLVD.

BROADWAY EXTENSION

CLASSEN BLVD.

NORTHWEST EXPY.

MAY AVE.

PENNSYLVANIA AVE.

North Canadian River

RENO AVE.

S. 15TH ST.

S. 29TH ST.

SHIELDS BLVD.

OKLAHOMA CITY
Downtown

warehouses, this area is filled with specialty shops and restaurants. You can also hop on the Water Taxi, which winds its way along the Bricktown Canal. When you're finished, settle down and rest—it's also a great place for people-watching!

Bricktown is a popular entertainment and dining district in Oklahoma City.

CHAPTER FIVE

THE PEOPLE AND PLACES OF OKLAHOMA

People from all backgrounds and all walks of life live in Oklahoma. According to the 2000 census, Oklahoma's population is 3,450,654. Almost 8 in every 10 people are of European descent. Within this group are people of German, Irish, Italian, and English heritage. Almost 8 in 100 people are African-American, in every 100 is Native American, and only 1 in 100 is Asian. Five in every 100 people are Hispanic (someone from Latin America living in the United States, especially people from Mexico, Puerto Rico, or Cuba).

Most Oklahomans live in busy metropolitan areas: Oklahoma City, Tulsa, Lawton, and Enid. Most of the state's largest cities are located near Oklahoma City or Tulsa. Some Native Americans live on land trusts—land that has been given to specific tribes by the United States government—while others live in towns with people from other backgrounds and cultures.

Visitors from all over the country come to Oklahoma City each year to celebrate Native American culture at the Red Earth Festival.

WORKING IN OKLAHOMA

Within the past two years, many new jobs have been created in Oklahoma. The majority of Oklahomans work in community, business, and personal service fields. Employers in this area include rental companies, telemarketing firms, and repair shops, among others.

The next largest employers are manufacturing companies, or companies that make machines or other products or equipment. Oil field machinery, construction machinery, machine parts, and refrigeration and heating equipment are some types of machinery made in Oklahoma. Manufacturing plants and factories are located in various parts of the state. Tulsa has plants that produce electronic components (parts), aircraft and aerospace equipment, and military communication systems. Factories in Oklahoma City produce products such as telephone equipment and tires.

Government activities employ the largest group of people. More than 300,000 Oklahomans work in this area, which includes public schools, hospitals, and military bases. The University of Oklahoma Health Sciences Center is one of the state's leading medical facilities. Tinker Air Force Base, located near Oklahoma City, is also one of the state's major employers.

Some Oklahomans work in the service industry as teachers.

56

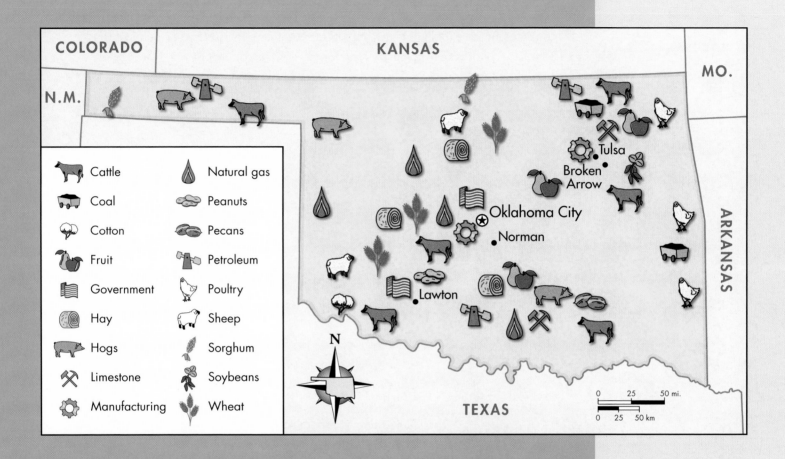

![Cattle]	Cattle	![Natural gas]	Natural gas
![Coal]	Coal	![Peanuts]	Peanuts
![Cotton]	Cotton	![Pecans]	Pecans
![Fruit]	Fruit	![Petroleum]	Petroleum
![Government]	Government	![Poultry]	Poultry
![Hay]	Hay	![Sheep]	Sheep
![Hogs]	Hogs	![Sorghum]	Sorghum
![Limestone]	Limestone	![Soybeans]	Soybeans
![Manufacturing]	Manufacturing	![Wheat]	Wheat

COLORADO

KANSAS

MO.

N.M.

Tulsa

Broken Arrow

Oklahoma City

Norman

Lawton

ARKANSAS

N

TEXAS

0   25   50 mi.

0   25   50 km

Nearly half the state's cropland produces wheat, and peanuts are mostly grown in the south-west part of the state. Both of these crops come together in this recipe for peanut bars, a delicious treat that is easy to make. Don't forget to ask an adult for help!

PEANUT BARS

vegetable oil cooking spray
1/2 cup smooth peanut butter
1/4 cup soft margarine
1 cup light brown sugar
2 large eggs
1-1/2 teaspoon vanilla extract
1 cup chopped salted peanuts
2/3 cup all-purpose flour

1. Preheat oven to 350 degrees. Spray 8-inch square baking pan with vegetable oil cooking spray.
2. Cream peanut butter with margarine in a medium-sized bowl until smooth.
3. Gradually add light brown sugar, beating until well blended.
4. Add eggs and continue to stir. Add vanilla extract.
5. Sift flour into small bowl and add to the peanut butter mixture. Fold in peanuts.
6. Pour batter into baking pan. Spread batter evenly with spatula.
7. Bake for 30 to 35 minutes and let cool for 15 minutes. Cut into 2-inch squares. Remove bars from pan with spatula and let them cool on a wire rack before serving. Makes 16 squares.

The mining industry employs about 28,000 Oklahomans. Natural gas, petroleum, coal, iodine, and gravel are some of the mineral products produced in the state. Oklahoma is the only state that produces iodine. Phillips Petroleum, one of the world's largest oil and gas companies, is located in Bartlesville.

Oklahoma has many farms and ranches. People working in this field are called farmers, ranchers, and cowhands. Although the number of farms in Oklahoma is increasing, the size of each farm is smaller than those in other states.

A champion bronc rider hangs on at the International Finals Youth Rodeo.

SPORTS AND RECREATION

Although Oklahoma has no major-league sports teams, Oklahomans take great pride in their athletes. NCAA Division 1 sports teams include Oklahoma State University's Cowboys, Oral Roberts University's Golden Eagles, the University of Oklahoma's Sooners, and the University of Tulsa's Golden Hurricanes. The state is also home to the Softball Hall of Fame in Oklahoma City and the National Wrestling Hall of Fame and Museum in Stillwater, where you can learn about wrestling champions nationwide, from the past to the present.

The rodeo is an exciting, popular sport in Oklahoma today. Some annual rodeo events include the

Youth Rodeo for cowboys and cowgirls, held each July in Shawnee; Guthrie's Bullnanza, where participants from around the world compete for a cash prize; and McAlester State Penitentiary's Prison Rodeo.

Oklahoma also has some unique sporting events, such as the World Cow Chip Throwing Championship. Every spring, folks from around the world gather in Beaver to see who can throw hard cow "dung" the farthest. It's a fun—and smelly—event!

Some of the greatest coaches and athletes who hail from Oklahoma include Jim Thorpe, one of the greatest athletes of all time; Heisman Memorial Trophy winners Billy Vessels, Steve Owens, and Billy Sims; Bud Wilkinson, the legendary college football coach; baseball Hall of Famer Micky Mantle; golfer Nancy Lopez Knight; Jim Shoulders, winner of sixteen rodeo championships; and Olympic gold medalist Shannon Miller.

TAKE A TOUR OF OKLAHOMA

Oklahoma is sometimes referred to as the land of six countries. These countries or regions include Green Country (northeast); Kiamichi Country (southeast); Lake and Trail Country (south central); Frontier Country (central) Great Plains Country (southwest); and Red Carpet Country (west and northwest). Let's begin our tour in northeastern Oklahoma.

Green Country

The northeast corner is called Green Country. There you will see the beautiful Tallgrass Prairie and the peaks of the Winding Stair Mountains.

Green Country has many parks and resorts. You can canoe along the lazy Illinois River or fish in one of the region's many beautiful streams.

Aside from the natural surroundings, there are lots of great sites to see in Green Country. Green Country's busiest city is Tulsa. Tulsa is home to the Philbrook Museum of Art and the Gilcrease Museum, both of which feature permanent special collections from around the globe. Bells Amusement Park and the Tulsa Zoo are also popular attractions.

South of Tulsa is Muskogee, where you can learn more about the history and culture of the Five Civilized Tribes at the Five Civilized Tribes Museum. The museum is housed in the historic Indian Agency building, which was built in 1875. Today, it is filled with art related to the area's rich Native American heritage, including pottery, baskets, beadwork, and paintings. In Claremore, stop at the Will Rogers Memorial Museum to find out more about one of Oklahoma's legendary cowboys.

Green Country also has many exciting annual events, such as the Juneteenth Heritage Festival. This festival, held each June, is a freedom celebration filled with historic speeches, parades, art exhibits, entertainment, and more. The International Balloon Festival, held in Gatesway, is another delight. Children and teens can build their own hot-air balloons made of tissue paper and watch them fly.

The Tallgrass Prairie is one of the few large tracts of unbroken prairieland left in the United States.

Robbers Cave State Park offered plenty of places for outlaws to hide back in the 1800s.

Kiamichi Country

Kiamichi Country is in southeast Oklahoma. There you will find the Kiamichi and Sans Bois mountains and the blue-tinged mountains of the Ouachita National Forest. This region is great for hiking. But be on the lookout! Long ago, outlaws used Kiamichi Country as a hiding place. The Dalton Gang and Belle Starr hid out in Robbers Cave State Park.

Kiamichi Country was once home to the Spiro Mound people. Spiro Mounds Archaeological Park is located near a city

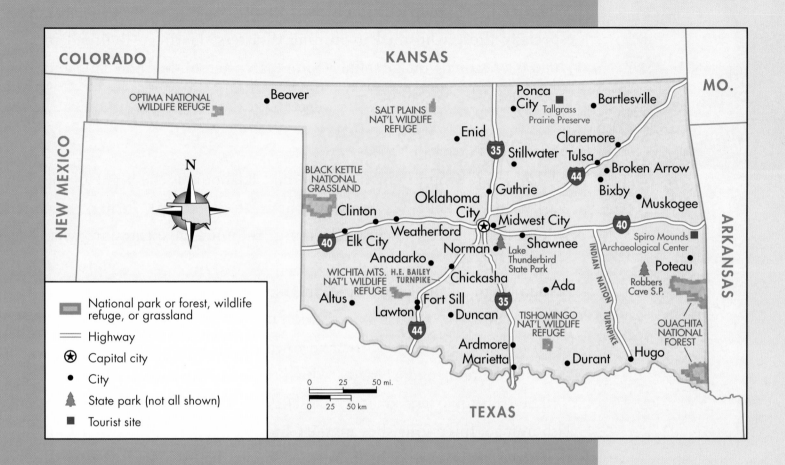

COLORADO

KANSAS

MO.

NEW MEXICO

OPTIMA NATIONAL
WILDLIFE REFUGE

Beaver

SALT PLAINS
NAT'L WILDLIFE
REFUGE

Ponca
City

Tallgrass
Prairie Preserve

Bartlesville

Enid

Claremore

N

Stillwater

Tulsa

BLACK KETTLE
NATIONAL
GRASSLAND

35

44

Broken Arrow

Guthrie

Bixby

Clinton

Oklahoma
City

Muskogee

Midwest City

40

Weatherford

Spiro Mounds
Archaeological Center

40

Elk City

Shawnee

Norman

ARKANSAS

Anadarko

Lake
Thunderbird
State Park

WICHITA MTS.
NAT'L WILDLIFE
REFUGE

H.E. BAILEY
TURNPIKE

Poteau

Chickasha

Ada

Robbers
Cave S.P.

Altus

Fort Sill

Lawton

35

TISHOMINGO
NAT'L WILDLIFE
REFUGE

OUACHITA
NATIONAL
FOREST

44

Duncan

Ardmore

Marietta

Durant

Hugo

0   25   50 mi.

0   25   50 km

TEXAS

Legend

National park or forest, wildlife
refuge, or grassland

Highway

⊛ Capital city

• City

🌲 State park (not all shown)

■ Tourist site

called Poteau. Other tourist attractions include the Pioneer Coal Miner Memorial in McAlester. It stands as a tribute to all miners in the area, especially those who died in mining disasters. Heritage Railroad in Hugo is a restored vintage train. Visitors can listen to the choo choo and think about the old railroad days.

Lake and Trail Country

Lake and Trail Country in south-central Oklahoma is the home of the Washita River, Lake Texoma, and the 77-foot (23-m) Turner Falls. Swimming, canoeing, or just relaxing in the mineral springs are what tourists enjoy most.

Ada is one of the largest cities in Lake and Trail Country. Incorporated in 1901, the city has a population of 15,691. Ada is home to East Central University. Other cities and towns in this area are Tishomingo, Durant, Ardmore, and Marietta, which is the county seat.

The headquarters of the Chickasaw Nation are located in Tishomingo. Interesting sites are the Chickasaw Bank Building, the Old Chickasaw capitol, and the Chickasaw Council House. Inside the council house is the original structure that contains the tribe's first written constitution from 1856. The first county courthouse built after statehood was granted, the Love County Courthouse, is located in Marietta. There is also the Love County Military Museum, which houses war memorabilia from the Civil War to the War on Terror. If you enjoy collecting dolls, there are more than 300 rare and antique dolls on display at the Eliza Cruce Hall Doll Museum in Ardmore.

Norman and Oklahoma City are the two largest and busiest cities in Frontier Country, or central Oklahoma. Norman has a population of 95,694. This city's growth and development stemmed from the establishment of the Santa Fe Railroad. Norman is home to the University of Oklahoma, the state's first institution of higher learning, which was created in 1890. One of Oklahoma's newest attractions, the Sam Noble Oklahoma Museum of Natural History, is located at the university. This museum is home to exhibits, artifacts, and information relating to the history, art, and culture of Oklahomans.

When you drive along the famous Route 66, you will see plenty of historic landmarks, including Oklahoma's only round wooden barn, built in 1898. This barn has been preserved over the years by caring community residents. Guthrie, Oklahoma's territorial capital from 1889 to

Downtown Guthrie is a National Historic Landmark because of its many restored eighteenth- and nineteenth-century buildings.

1910, has some interesting highlights that include the Capital Publishing Museum and Oklahoma's Territorial Museum. One of Guthrie's annual sports events is Bullnanza, held each February. Some of the toughest cowboys from around the world compete against one another during this event.

Frontier Country is also home to the air and space museum, called the Omniplex, which houses seven museums under one roof; and the National Cowboy and Western Heritage Museum, both in Oklahoma City. Other cities and towns located in Frontier Country include Guthrie, Edmond, Langston, and Seminole. Boley and Langston, two historic African-American towns, are now the site of historic buildings and African-American heritage exhibits.

Great Plains Country

Great Plains Country was once the home of the Kiowa and Comanche tribes, who were great buffalo hunters. Now, buffalo and other animals live in the 60,000-acre (24,000-ha) Wichita Mountains National Wildlife Refuge.

Oklahoma's great forts are located in Lawton. Fort Sill is currently a major military outpost. It once served as the United States Army's

Exhibits relating to the history of fort and field artillery are on display at the Fort Sill Museum.

headquarters during the Indian War. It was also a prison camp where many Comanche and Kiowa chiefs served time.

If you drive along U.S. Highway 81, imagine that you are living in the late 1800s and that you are driving cattle instead of a car. Great Plains Country museums include the Museum of the Great Plains, which has a reproduction of the Red River Trading Post, complete with fur trappers, traders, and their goods; and the General Thomas P. Stafford Airport Museum (Weatherford), a museum that highlights the life and times of astronaut and Oklahoma native Thomas Stafford. The Oklahoma Route 66 Museum in Clinton highlights the eight states that lay along this famous road. Elk City's Old Town Museum Complex

WHO'S WHO IN OKLAHOMA?

Black Beaver (1806–1880) served as an interpreter for the exploratory expedition under General Henry Leavenworth and Colonel Henry Dodge to the Upper Red River Territory in 1834. This territory was home to the Plains Indians. Black Beaver served as a Union scout during the Civil War and later became a spokesperson for his tribe during negotiations. Black Beaver died at Anadarko on the Washita River in Indian Territory.

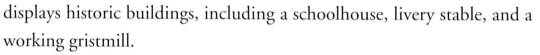

displays historic buildings, including a schoolhouse, livery stable, and a working gristmill.

The city of Anadarko, founded in 1901, is in the southwest part of Great Plains Country. Anadarko can best be described as the center of Native American culture and activities. The National Hall of Fame for Famous American Indians houses information about Sequoyah and Captain Black Beaver, as well as other American Indian leaders. Other cities and towns in Great Plains Country include Altus and Duncan.

Red Carpet Country

Red Carpet Country's deep-red soil resulted from the vast prehistoric sea that once covered the Panhandle area. This region includes sand dunes more than 40 feet (12 m) high and the lava-covered Black Mesa. You may also find some dinosaur tracks there.

Interesting attractions in this area include Leonardo's Discovery Warehouse and the Adventure Quest in Enid, a huge hands-on museum and playground. There is also the Shattuck Windmill Museum, where numerous windmills from the early settler days are displayed. Don't miss the statue of the Pioneer Woman in Ponca City, which stands 17 feet (5 m) and weighs 12,000 pounds (5,400 kilograms). To the east of the statue is the Pioneer Woman Museum. This museum preserves the legacy of women from all races, creeds, and nationalities who have contributed to Oklahoma's development.

This bronze pioneer statue in Ponca City honors the many women who played a part in the development of Oklahoma.

PIONEER WOMAN

OKLAHOMA ALMANAC

Statehood date and number: November 16, 1907; 46th state

State seal: Features a five-pointed star containing the symbols of the Five Civilized Tribes. The upper-left point has a small star with a wreath of oak leaves, the symbol of the Cherokee Nation. The center point has the symbol of the Chickasaw Nation, a warrior with a bow and shield. The upper-right point has the emblem of the Choctaw Nation—a tomahawk, bow, and three crossed arrows. The Seminole Nation is represented by a house and a factory beside a lake and a Native American in a canoe. The sheaf of wheat and plow in the lower-left point represents the Creek Nation. The surrounding smaller stars represent the other states in the Union in 1907. Adopted in 1907.

State flag: The background of the state flag is blue, symbolizing loyalty and devotion. In the center of the flag is the buckskin shield of the Osage warrior. Two symbols of peace, on the olive branch and a peace pipe, cross the shield. The word *Oklahoma* was added in 1941. Adopted in 1925.

Geographic center: 8 miles (13 km) north of Oklahoma City

Total area/rank: 69,919 square miles (181,089 sq km)/18th

Borders: Kansas, Arkansas, Texas, Colorado, New Mexico, Missouri

Latitude and longitude: Oklahoma is located approximately between 33° 38' and 37° 00' N and 94° 26' and 103° 00' W

Highest/lowest elevation: Black Mesa, 4,973 feet (1,516 m) above sea level/287 feet (87 m) above sea level along the Little River

Hottest/coldest temperature: 120° F (49° C) at Alva on July 18, 1936; at Altus, July 19 and August 12, 1936; at Poteau on August 10, 1936; at Tishomingo, July 26, 1943; and at Tipton, June 27, 1994/–27° F (–33° C) at Vinita, Feb. 13, 1905, and at Watts, January 18, 1930

Land area/rank: 68,695 square miles (177,919 sq km)/19th

Inland water area/rank: 1,224 square miles (3,171 sq km)/17th

Population/rank: 3,450,654 (2000 census)/27th

Population of major cities:

Oklahoma City: 506,132

Tulsa: 393,049

Norman: 95,694

Lawton: 92,757

Broken Arrow: 74,859

Origin of state name: Combination of two Choctaw Indian words: *okl,* meaning "people," and *humma,* meaning "red"

State capital: Oklahoma City

Previous capital: Guthrie

Counties: 77

State government: 48 senators, 101 representatives

Major rivers/lakes: Arkansas River, Canadian River, Red River, North Canadian/Lake Eufaula

Farm products: Winter wheat, cotton, dairy products, peanuts, soybeans, hay, grain, sorghum

Livestock: Beef cattle, poultry, hogs

Manufactured products: Oil field machinery; construction machinery; machine parts; refrigeration and heating equipment; structural metal, aircraft and aerospace equipment communication systems; television parts; telephone equipment; transportation equipment; food products (baked goods, meat products, and soft drinks); fabricated metal products; rubber and plastic products; tires

Mining products: Natural gas, petroleum, coal, crushed stone, limestone, sand, gravel, iodine, zinc, cement, and silver

Amphibian: Bullfrog

Animal: Bison

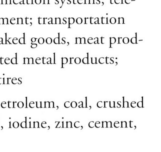

Beverage: Milk

Bird: Scissor-tailed flycatcher

Butterfly: Black swallowtail

Colors: Green and white

Fish: White, or sand, bass

Flower: Mistletoe

Folk dance: Square dance

Furbearer: Raccoon

Game animal: White-tailed deer

Grass: Indian grass

Insect: Honey bee

Motto: *Labor Omnia Vincit* (Labor Conquers All Things)

Musical Instrument: Fiddle

Nicknames: Sooner State, Boomer State, America's Frontier Lake State, Land of Six Countries

Poem: "Howdy Folks," by David Randolph Milsten

Reptile: Mountain boomer lizard

Rock: Barite rose (rose rock)

Song: "Oklahoma!" music by Richard Rodgers; words by Oscar Hammerstein, II

Tree: Redbud

Waltz: "Oklahoma Wind"

Wildflower: Indian blanket

Wildlife: Deer, armadillos, coyotes, raccoons, prairie dogs, cottontails, jackrabbits, gray and fox squirrels, mink, opossums, gray and red foxes, skunks, otters, antelope, copperhead snakes, cottonmouth

snakes, rattlesnakes, crows, blue jays, cardinals, warblers, crows, doves, swallows, meadowlarks, mockingbirds, robins, scissor-tailed flycatchers, orioles, killdeers, English sparrows, red-winged blackbirds, quail, pheasant, wild turkeys, cattle egrets, cowbirds, green and little blue herons, and roadrunners

TIMELINE

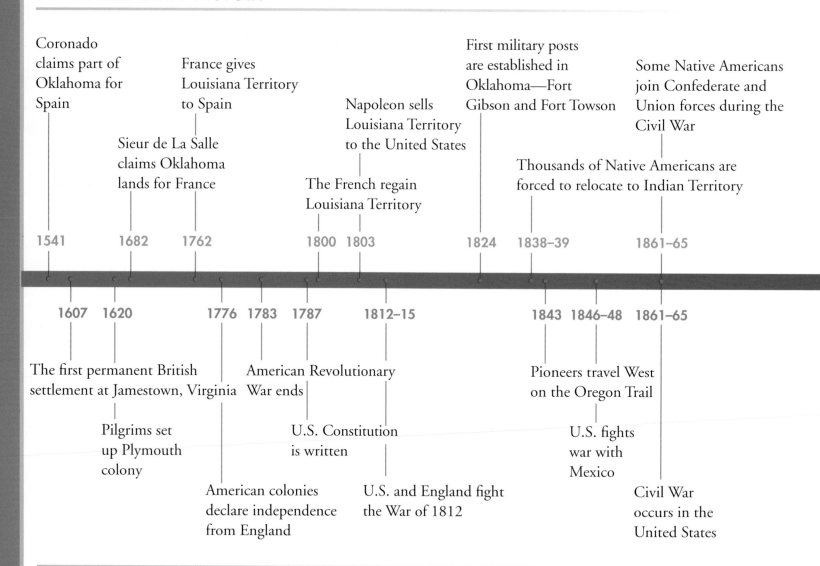

OKLAHOMA STATE HISTORY

Coronado claims part of Oklahoma for Spain

Sieur de La Salle claims Oklahoma lands for France

France gives Louisiana Territory to Spain

Napoleon sells Louisiana Territory to the United States

The French regain Louisiana Territory

First military posts are established in Oklahoma—Fort Gibson and Fort Towson

Thousands of Native Americans are forced to relocate to Indian Territory

Some Native Americans join Confederate and Union forces during the Civil War

| 1541 | 1682 | 1762 | 1800 | 1803 | 1824 | 1838–39 | 1861–65 |

| 1607 | 1620 | 1776 | 1783 | 1787 | 1812–15 | 1843 | 1846–48 | 1861–65 |

The first permanent British settlement at Jamestown, Virginia

Pilgrims set up Plymouth colony

American Revolutionary War ends

American colonies declare independence from England

U.S. Constitution is written

U.S. and England fight the War of 1812

Pioneers travel West on the Oregon Trail

U.S. fights war with Mexico

Civil War occurs in the United States

UNITED STATES HISTORY

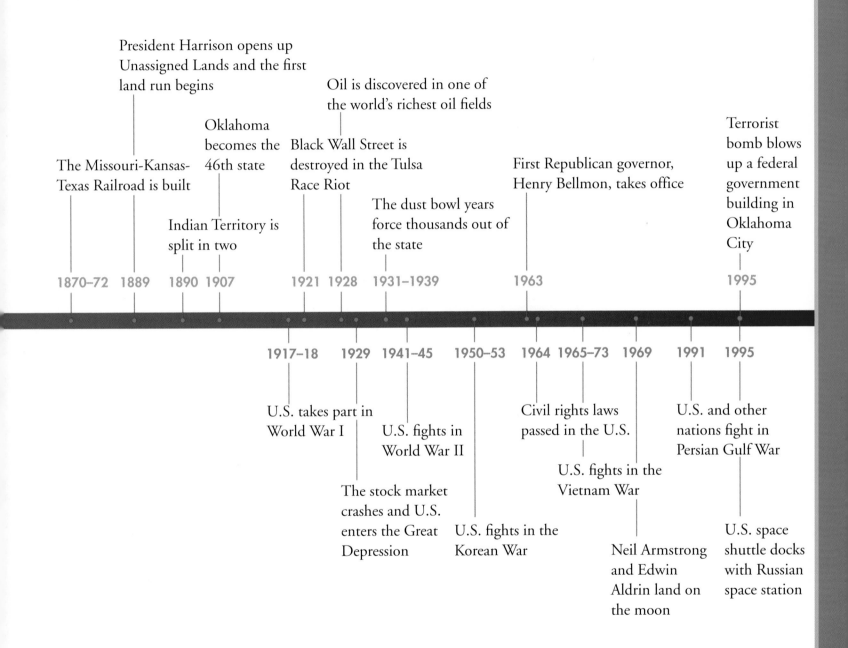

President Harrison opens up
Unassigned Lands and the first
land run begins

Oil is discovered in one of
the world's richest oil fields

Oklahoma
becomes the
46th state

Black Wall Street is
destroyed in the Tulsa
Race Riot

Terrorist
bomb blows
up a federal
government
building in
Oklahoma
City

The Missouri-Kansas-
Texas Railroad is built

First Republican governor,
Henry Bellmon, takes office

The dust bowl years
force thousands out of
the state

Indian Territory is
split in two

1870–72   1889   1890   1907   1921   1928   1931–1939   1963   1995

1917–18   1929   1941–45   1950–53   1964   1965–73   1969   1991   1995

U.S. takes part in
World War I

Civil rights laws
passed in the U.S.

U.S. and other
nations fight in
Persian Gulf War

U.S. fights in
World War II

U.S. fights in the
Vietnam War

The stock market
crashes and U.S.
enters the Great
Depression

U.S. fights in the
Korean War

Neil Armstrong
and Edwin
Aldrin land on
the moon

U.S. space
shuttle docks
with Russian
space station

GALLERY OF FAMOUS OKLAHOMANS

Johnny Bench (Lee)
(1947–)
Baseball player, part Cherokee. Bench hit 389 career home runs for the Cincinnati Reds and was elected to the Baseball Hall of Fame in 1989. Born in Oklahoma City.

Garth Brooks
(1962–)
Popular country-western music star. Born in Tulsa.

Floyd Cooper
(1959–)
Award-winning children's book illustrator. Cooper received a Coretta Scott King Award for the illustrations in *Brown Honey in Broomwheat Tea*. Born in Tulsa.

Vince Gill
(1957–)
Country singer, songwriter, and guitarist. He won five consecutive Country Music Association Awards for best male vocalist. He also won fourteen Grammy Awards. Born in Norman.

Shannon Lucid
(1943–)
Astronaut and biochemist. She set a new record for the longest mission in space (188 days) and was the first woman to be awarded the Congressional Space Medal of Honor. Born in China and raised in Bethany.

Leona Mitchell
(1949–)
A well-known opera star. Born in Enid.

Bill Moyers
(1934–)
Well-known television journalist. He has produced more than 200 hours of informational programming. Born in Hugo.

Daniel Patrick Moynihan
(1927–2003)
Politician and academic. He served in the administrations of Presidents Johnson and Nixon and was the author of a famous report in 1965 called *The Negro Family: The Case for National Action*. This report helped focus national attention on the problems of African-American families. Born in Tulsa.

Brad Pitt
(1963–)
Television and film actor. *Fight Club* and *Sleepers* are two of the many movies he has starred in. Born in Shawnee.

Oral Roberts
(1918–)
World-famous television evangelist. He founded Oral Roberts University in Tulsa. Born in Ada.

GLOSSARY

abolish: to officially put an end to something

adopt: to accept an idea or recommendation

archaeologist: a person who studies ancient artifacts to learn about the past

artifact: a simple, man-made object that is evidence of an early culture

bill: the draft of a proposed new law

convicted: to be proven guilty

engineer: a person who is trained to design and build vehicles, machines, bridges, roads, and other structures

erosion: the wearing away of land by water, wind, or ice

evangelist: a preacher of the Christian gospel

fort: building that is strongly built to endure attacks

herd: to make animals or people move together in a group

homesteader: a settler who receives and farms land under the Homestead Act

hydroelectric: the production of electricity by water power

judicial: having to do with a court of law or a judge

meteorologist: a person who studies the Earth's atmosphere to make weather predictions

mound: a man-made hill or heap of earth, sometimes built over a burial site

neutral: not siding with either of two opposing sides in a dispute

pioneer: one of the first people to explore or settle on new land or territory

prehistoric: related to the period before recorded history

slave: person who is owned by another person and performs hard work for no pay and has no freedom

treaty: a signed agreement or contract

unconstitutional: something that is not permitted by the Constitution

FOR MORE INFORMATION

Web sites

Oklahoma Governor

http://www.governor.state.ok.us/

The official Web site of the governor of Oklahoma.

TravelOK

http://www.travelok.com/

The official Web site of the Oklahoma Tourism and Recreation Department.

CyberSleuth Kids

http://cybersleuth-kids.com/sleuth/Geography/United_States/Oklahoma/index.htm

Links to Web sites about Oklahoma history, geography, government, and interesting places.

Books

Bruchac, Joseph and Diana Magnuson. *Trail of Tears.* New York: Random House, 1999.

Ross, Jim, ed. *Dear Oklahoma City, Get Well Soon.* New York: Walker and Co, 1996.

Sanford, William R. *The Chisholm Trail in American History.* Berkeley Heights, NJ: Enslow Publishers, 2000.

Smith Baranzini, Marlene and Howard Egger-Bovet. *USKids History: Book of the American Indians.* Boston: Little, Brown and Company, 1994.

Stein, R. Conrad. *The Oklahoma City National Memorial.* Danbury, CT: Children's Press, 2003.

Addresses

Governor of Oklahoma

Room 212
State Capitol Building
Oklahoma City, OK 73105

Oklahoma Arts Council

2101 N. Lincoln Boulevard, Room 640
Oklahoma City, OK 73105

Oklahoma Tourism and Recreation

15 N. Robinson Street, Suite 801
Oklahoma City, OK 73105

INDEX

ABOUT THE AUTHOR

Linda Saylor-Marchant is manager of the Cooper River Memorial Library of the Charleston County Library System. She holds a B.S. degree in business administration and personnel management from York College, City University of New York; and a master's degree in library science from the University of Pittsburgh. She lives with her three children, Garth Jr., Aziza, and Eleanor, in Summerville, South Carolina.